Cura Te Ipsum

Integrative Critique: On Combining Adlerian,

Existential, and Rational Emotive Behavioral Theory

in Psychotherapy

Hannah L. Roles

Contents

Abstract

Existential psychology, Adler's psychoanalytic approach and Ellis rational emotive behavioral therapy have a number of things in common. Each of these approaches expects the client to find health through making the choice to change self-perception and then acting accordingly. Living in the present and maintaining a factual view of the world is a key component to each one of these approaches, whether as the end-goal or a means to the end. Existential psychology represents the individual, Adler's work represents the interpersonal, and Ellis's theoretical framework supplies the structure that grounds these three approaches. A plausible integration of these models is presented here, with theory of personality, psychopathology, therapeutic process, shortcomings and strengths outlined in clear language. It is noted that this paper is simply a presentation. Research is necessary to validate this integration and would lend valuable understanding to its suggested application.

Integrative Critique: On Combining Adlerian, Existential, and Rational Emotive Behavioral Theory in Psychotherapy

Alfred Adler once stated that "a man is not determined by his environment, but by his estimate of it (Rozsnafzsky, 1974)." This is a central tenant in the current practice of psychotherapy, although opinions range about whether that estimation is based on past experience or if it is based on mans' understanding of that experience. In conducting psychotherapy, the practitioner looks for a therapeutic model that is well rounded, effective, and appropriate for the client, whoever the client may be. Unfortunately, no therapy model exists that answers this need for every client. The human condition being unique as it is, it has become necessary for therapists to blend elements from different models in order to create a tool kit broad enough to 'fix' the problem, but sensitive enough to process the details.

Ellis's rational emotive behavioral therapy (REBT) is an effective, scientifically validated model that itself draws on other theorist's work (Groth, 2006; Prochaska & Norcross, 2010; Whitfield, 2006). It has been stated that Adler's psychodynamic theory is one of the building blocks for Ellis's work (Rozsnafzsky, 1974), but with its candid social interest, presents a very different but integrate-able method. Existential psychology, with its rich understanding of the human condition and habit-of-mind approach to change, is more of a philosophy than a therapy model. However, it presents ideas that are unique within the field of psychology and, when applied with care, have the potential to improve upon both the therapist's approach to treatment and the client's ability to use it.

Theory of Personality

Existentialism.

Philosopher Martin Heidegger first used the term 'dasein' to refer to the human existence. When translated literally from German, it means 'being here' (Daitz, 2011). Ludwig Binswanger, Medard Boss, and Rollo May all relied heavily on Heidegger's philosophy, and thus had no problem adopting his terms in their pursuit of existential psychology. Existentialists cast the human condition in this way. Man is inseparable from the world around him because he is responsible for creating his own world and his own existence. This is a world-changing concept that is anchored on three points. The Umwelt, or being-in-the-world, is how human beings relate to all things physical and biological.

The Mitwelt, or being-with-others, is the place in the world where man relates to his fellow man. Friendships, marriages, and therapeutic relationships fall in this realm. The Eigenwelt, or being-with-self, is that part of man's existence where he relates to himself. Ideally, a person is honest enough with himself to maintain balance in all three of these worlds. Such a person is considered fully, existentially conscious (Groth, 2010).

This balance is what Binswanger first described as 'authenticity.' An authentic person does not shy from reality, and makes the choice to examine each part of it. In existential terms, this is perfect mental health. Having an authentic view of the world allows will allow human beings to act in an accurate, honest manner without fear of judgment or censure. Authentic people are aware that there is much more to their existence than what other people think of them. They know that they are going to make

mistakes, and that it is perfectly normal to be concerned about those mistakes. Their fulfillment comes from living an unlocked, open life.

Even unlocked lives are rife with what Boss and May referred to as existential anxiety. This anxiety manifests for good reason; human beings are naturally afraid of death, a life without meaning, and taking action where risk is present (Prochaska & Norcross, 2010). The difference between a healthy person and an unhealthy person, then, is how they choose to deal with that anxiety. While the conscious person is aware of these anxieties and what causes them, the unconscious person goes through life often ruled by them. At this point, unconscious people have a choice. They can step away from the pattern of existence they have been maintaining and attempt to find the cause of the anxiety, or they can lie to themselves about it. Lying to oneself is necessary for the survival of an unconscious life, and existentialists believe that it is the base of all psychopathology (Canning, 2001).

Adlerian Psychology.

Adler was less concerned with a balanced life and more concerned with an active one. He believed that all human beings were born feeling inferior to the task of living, and so combated that fear by striving for superiority. He did not mean that they were striving for superiority over one another, but that they were attempting to create the most complete version of themselves. This, in Adler's view, is a necessary component of life and is not something to shrink from. He believed that a child's social history within his family would define the path that person took to superiority. Birth order, parenting, and what Adler called 'organ inferiority' are of particular importance because they are directly tied to how a child processes what he can expect from the world.

Organ inferiority refers to a child's genetic endowment and any physical tendencies they may have. He believed that an organ inferiority could either work for or against a developing child, depending on how healthy the environment they were raised in was. For example, Adler suffered from rickets as a child, and it left him with a lifelong impairment in mobility. He did not allow this to stop him from touring Europe and the United States while promoting his brand of psychotherapy (Mosak & Fasula, 2011).

Birth order was the basis for a child's social endowment. Eldest children, dethroned from the beginning, are high achievers with a desire to please. Middle children rebel against the rules and expectations so faithfully adhered to by their older siblings. Youngest children, while measuring their own development against that of their older siblings, often never leave the favored position the oldest child has long since vacated. All of these dynamics can lead to different forms of inferiority complexes, and thus define the personal drives of each person.

Extreme permissiveness or rigidity from parents defines personality just as clearly. A permissive parent, allowing the child to live at his own whim and shielding him from necessary responsibilities (learning to work, learning to interact with different types of people, etc.) teach this child that not only is he incapable of living under his own auspices, but that he should expect assistance throughout life. A rigid parent teaches the same incapability, but it comes about for a very different reason. Children raised in a

rigid, controlling household learn that they are incapable not because they need help, but because they are unworthy. In either of these conditions, these children are likely to make what Alder referred to as 'basic mistakes' when constructing their lifestyles, and psychopathology is the result (Kummerow & Maguire, 2010).

REBT.

In contrast with the preceding therapies, Ellis believed personality was a very loose concept based almost entirely in the present. An activating event (A) creates a belief (B), and the action upon that belief results in a consequence (C). He believed that consistency in behavior came from a particular belief system, and that it is not the outside world that defined us, as Adler believed, but what is on the inside (Prochaska & Norcross, 2010; Groth, 2010). People are psychologically healthy or not based on how rational their belief systems are. Absolutism creates irrational beliefs. Irrational beliefs lead to psychopathology. As children, it is very easy for human beings to function as if the world is black and white, in part because our cognitive abilities cannot process the world in any other way. Absolutism survives in an adult because it is simple easier than looking at the more complex reality of the world. If a person maintains an absolutist view of the world --- "I should be able to finish my work more quickly than my younger siblings,"; "I need that 2012-model Camaro!"--- then that person is going to develop psychopathological symptoms.

Integration.

Little is borrowed from Adler's personality theory in this integration, except to acknowledge the profound effect family dynamics and the mind-body connection have on the development of personality. It is a mistake to confine personality development entirely to the external elements of the world or the internal ones, but rather, both of these pieces are necessary for development. Ellis's rational approach to personality development can be overlaid with the concepts of Umwelt, Mitwelt, and Eigenwelt to create a clearer understanding of our personalities.

For example, we know that epigenetics plays a powerful role in the genetic expression of infants. If a pregnant woman carries her child in a war zone, that child will be born with a genetic tendency toward heightened physical arousal because of the high stress load his mother experienced while she was carrying him. If prenatal development is the activating event in a child's life, then his beliefs are going to be shaped by his innate biological tendencies, or his Umwelt. If this child's beliefs are informed by his inborn tendency toward alertness, then the consequences of his actions are going to be directly linked to his expressed genetic framework. Even if he and his mother escape the war zone and he grows up in a peaceful environment, both this child's beliefs about how he relates to other people and his beliefs about himself are tied in to that single activating event; his genetic endowment due to his conception and birth in a war zone. His behavior and health can be tracked by Ellis's framework, ABC contingency by ABC contingency, but it cannot be explained or fully managed if all a therapist looks at is his present belief system. The contingency framework is marvelous, however, when, full acknowledgement of his biological make-up in mind, this young client begins to learn how to manage his anger in a positive manner instead of acting out. If he is conscious of his Umwelt, then he will be able to recognize that unnecessary alertness before it ever leads to unconscious action.

Psychopathology

Existentialism.

As stated above, untruths are the cause of psychopathology. When a person is presented with a genuine reason for anxiety and they choose to lie, either in the service of themselves or in the service of others, neurotic anxiety results (Smith, 2000). The author's late grandmother provided one of the clearest examples of neurotic anxiety in the author's experience. Mrs. A. C. was a breast cancer survivor who lived for nearly twenty years past her initial diagnosis. The truth of her situation was that she had every reason to live freely, but she was fearful that every ache and illness was a sign that her cancer was coming out of remission. When faced with the very real chances of her death at her initial diagnosis, Mrs. A. C. chose not to carry on with her survival but lived in great fear of her own humanity. Instead of choosing to take advantage of the time she had, she chose to live in fear of having no time left at all. She never developed full-blown hypochondriasis, but a number of other compulsive behaviors sprung up in addition to her fear of illnesses. By the time doctors discovered spots of cancer on her spine and skull, she was under so much self imposed stress that her body was only too willing to shut down. Mrs. A. C. chose to lie in the service of her own inauthentic existence rather than tell herself the truth. She did so in part because she believed that the existence she had created was all that she had. Mrs. A. C. was an exceptional woman in many ways, but the most profound lesson the author learned from her was that lying to protect an unfounded assumption is one of the few human behaviors that will almost certainly lead to death.

Lying-in-the-service-of-self is done of our own volition. It pertains directly to how we see our world and allows us to maintain an inauthentic life.

We choose to maintain such a life out of fear, either of the unknown or the misperceived. It is the most difficult form of psychopathology to root out and usually the most persistent. The second form of lying, lying-in-the-service-of-others, involves deliberately misrepresenting ourselves to others to gain favor, social standing, or acceptance. These types of lies are often co-morbid, and as is the nature of lies, they tend to feed off of one another.

Adlerian Psychology.

Adler's notion of psychopathology ties directly to the framework of our childhood and the manner in which our parents raised us. If we were raised in a healthy household, we would be willing, energetic members of society. People raised in an abusive household become vengeful, antisocial individuals bent on exacting revenge from society. People raised in neglectful homes are self-defeating. People raised in pampering environments are lazy and expect assistance in all aspects of their lives. Adler believed that these frameworks led individuals from less-than-ideal backgrounds to make generalizations about the way society works based on their very small field of experience, and thus make what he termed basic mistakes in the building of their own styles of life (Prochaska & Norcross, 2010). He believed that if these distorted perceptions could be dispelled, then a person could easily see the goodness and kindness present in the world at large.

REBT.

Ellis also believed that psychopathology was, in part, the product of generalizations. More concisely, he believed that rigid, irrational thinking led to belief systems that simply did not work. It did not matter how much insight a person had into their childhood horrors if that person was still behaving in a manner that allowed for no improvement in psychological health. An activating event, usually occurring early in life, leads a person to develop an irrational belief. Once that belief is held, the person will continue to act on it as if it is true. For example, if a drunken parent screams at a child for no reason, the child may come to believe that he or she is simply bad, because otherwise the parent would have no reason for screaming. Based on that belief—'I am bad"—the child will either withdraw or act out, making good on the belief they've latched onto. This sort of cycle exists for every belief, whether rational or irrational. However, the problem with irrational beliefs is that they can become their own activating events. For example, a child may act out in a classroom setting simply because he believes he is bad. An alcoholic may continue to drink because he believes getting sober is a hopeless enterprise. The cycle continues, and psychopathology prevails (Matlin, 2009).

Integration.

All of these approaches rely in misperception in order for psychopathology to occur. The only one that lays the responsibility for psychopathology at the feet of the client is existential psychology. The only one that pays attention to detailed historical information is, unsurprisingly, Adlerian psychology. While the historical element is deeply important to fixing the problem, attributing psychopathology solely to child-hood environments is both narrow and unsupported. REBT takes an almost behaviorist viewpoint, and in this case, it is the element that best leads the integration. History is important, but an understanding of how psychopathology develops is best served by a behavioral map and an honest presentation of responsibility.

Therapeutic Process

The largest variation in therapy outcome is linked directly to elements the client brings with him to the session; the severity of any pre-existing mental conditions and his expectations of success (Prochaska & Norcross, 2010). The next most powerful element, however, is the client-therapist relationship. At its very core, psychotherapy is an interpersonal relationship. This is why, in part, that people are more willing to seek help for mental disorders from a priest or a close friend than they are from a psychologist. The basis is the same. REBT and Adlerian psychology strongly emphasize a teacher-student relationship, while existentialism stands quietly by, offering support but not assistance as the client learns to take responsibility for his way of living.

Existentialism.

The most esoteric of these three, existentialism leaves it up to the therapist and the client to ascertain how to raise and maintain consciousness. In some ways, this is as much the end goal of the existential psychology as authenticity is. Because it finds its roots in psychoanalysis, what little structure exists in this therapy is very similar to it (Wilberg, 2011). The client is encouraged to 'free-experience,' in the beginning of therapy. This means that the client is given implicit permission from the therapist, at least during therapy, to be whatever he may want to be. Because reality and perception are often difficult to reconcile, this is usually confined to a verbal representation of that desire. This is very similar to Freud's free association, but it begins in the present. It is absolutely client guided. The notion is that the client will tell the therapist, through free-experience where their psychological problems lie because he is imposing his own framework onto his perception of the therapy. For example, if a client has a problem with the way he relates to his physical world (his Umwelt), that problem will come up in the free-experience. If a gifted young scientist has always felt physically clumsy, he will speak of it. If a single mother has distanced herself from other people (Mitwelt), she will explain that distance. If a priest is struggling with a crisis of his faith (Eigenwelt) that titanic struggle will present itself in the course of free-experience (Batchelder, 2006).

And it is here, startlingly, that the structure of existential psychology ends. Once the imbalance is pinpointed, peeling back the inauthentic behavior that lead to the client's imbalance becomes a creative process between the client and therapist. They are cast as honest equals, although if the client is dealing with an imbalance across his worlds, honesty may not come easily at first. Clarity on the therapist's part is just as uncomfortable for the therapist as it is for the client, but this is one of the few areas where the therapist must lead by example. Such stark honesty requires risk from the therapist, and as the client realizes this through continued exposure to it, he can begin to feel safe taking such risks himself (Prochaska & Norcross, 2010). At this point, it is up to the client, processing his world with the help of the therapist's blunt feedback, to find his authentic self. If that authentic self is so cancer ridden that death is the preferable option, an existential therapist will not stand in the way. If that authentic self is gifted enough to sing The Phantom's part in The Phantom of the Opera but struggles with deep social anxiety, then the therapist will support every honest improvement in the Mitwelt. And when the client reaches an authentic understanding of his worth and talent, the therapist will stand cheering on the front row when the client sings that part on Broadway.

Adlerian Psychology.

Mozdzierez (2011) quotes Adler as follows: "The task of the….psychologist is to give the patient experience of contact with a fellow man and then enable him to transfer this awakened social interest to others." While existential psychology approaches the human condition as if each person is a whole unit, Adler posits that humankind is worth nothing if its members cannot function as that whole.

A healthy person, he believed, was a person who embraced a role in life that allowed him or her to create the most social good. If human beings do not add to the whole on an individual level, then they have failed as human beings. With this in mind, Adler paid close attention to the family history, creating a lifestyle analysis with the client. Using the client's social history as a baseline, Adler believed he could determine where the client's social deficits were and would then supply information to fill in the gaps. This included assigned readings (we owe the self-help book to Adler and his colleagues), social homework of any kind – attending a dance, creating pleasure in the life of another person ten times in a week, etc. -- , and confident, prosocial feedback from the therapist on each of these exercises. While Adler's psychodynamic approach could be defined as a depth theory, he implemented it in a very active fashion.

We have all heard the statement 'fake it 'til you make it.' While Adler did not coin that phrase precisely, he did use that notion as a large part of his therapy. He believed that if a client had difficulty laughing at himself, then the client should role-play as an individual who was routinely laughed at, like a clown, while in the safety of a therapy session. By practicing with unfamiliar emotional content, the client could come to understand what sort of change needed to be made in their own behavior in order to reach a more balanced psychological state.

REBT.

Ellis, like the existentialists, treats human beings as if they are their own whole units. The focus, however, is not on how honestly the client views the world, but how rationally. Ellis believed that our own inner workings were the culprit for any psychopathology. Humankind has just as much an attraction to the irrational as the rational, in part because it protects vulnerable pieces of our psyche or allows us to be cognitively lazy.

Ellis's notion is thus: irrationality can be its own activating event and its own consequence, which creates a horrid cycle of psychopathology. If a depressed person despairs because he cannot seem to get out of the 'funk' he is in, then that depression has served as the activating event for the shift from moderate to clinical depression. The piece in the middle then, is Ellis's focus. Why does the client believe that he cannot get out of the cycle? What about his existence is telling him that he does not have the capability to rise above his depression? It is the belief that needs dealt with, not the consequence or the event. His approach is simple: tear down the irrational belief and help the client reach a new, more effective philosophy.

This is where the student/teacher element of REBT becomes most evident. The client role is not unlike the role of a college freshman; "You have much to learn, but ask questions as often as you are able, because you have the capability to reach my level as professor, and in fact, may one day surpass me." They do homework, present their ideas to the therapist only to have them pushed back, narrowed, refined, and brought forth again as a more rational presentation of the circumstances they are living in. When the client has come to a clear understanding of their own irrational tendencies, it was not uncommon for Ellis to ask them to proctor small groups of people also seeking REBT therapy and have them teach it as a course! (Prochaska & Norcross, 2010) This is not unlike a graduate student taking a TA position and finding, upon teaching an entry level class, that a person truly does not understand what he knows until he has taught it to someone else.

Integration.

Each of these theoretical frameworks presents a different view on how one's personality develops. Adler tells us that people should devote their lives to becoming something more than they already are --- striving for superiority. Binswanger, Boss, and May suggest that an authentic, honest understanding of life is enough for a healthy individual (Smith, 2000). Ellis would have us step out into our lives as hedonists, simple as A-B-C (Prochaska & Norcross, 2010). At first blush, this does not a good cocktail make.

So why does the author believe that it works? First, the only real integration of method comes between Adler's psychodynamic theory and Ellis's rational emotive

behavior therapy. True to its psychoanalytic roots, Adler's therapy model maintains a deep interest in a client's past history, and there are points in therapy where this is a necessary focus. However, there is consternation in the psychological community about Adler's belief that only past history defines a person's behavior (Bitter & Main, 2011). Conversely, Ellis's work directly confronts the troubling present behavior long before it makes a concerted effort to understand the past history. Rationality, it would seem, should be enough to create and maintain mental stability. The truth of the matter is somewhere between these points. While we can say with a substantial amount of certainty that destroying irrational beliefs and replacing them with effective ones creates mental health (Prochaska & Norcross, 2010; Groth, 2010), a stubborn tendency to pay little attention to history does the client no favors. Birth order matters, especially in large families. So do childhood injuries and successes. While a client can only be held responsible for historical elements that he or she directly caused, these can still be painful to discuss.

Therefore, if an element much like Adler's lifestyle analysis were included at the beginning of treatment, the author feels it would prime the client for more rational thought regarding his life and beliefs before the therapist starts guiding him toward his present irrationality. It is practice, at a safe distance, for the client to begin analyzing himself and his own thought patterns. This could create a smoother transition into the meat of confrontations. If the client is less resistant toward the concept because of the previous scaffolding provided by the lifestyle analysis, he will be able to face his irrationalities with greater honesty because he already knows that he is capable of this line of thought.

Ordinarily, these two pieces of theory do not dovetail. If, however, a balance can be struck between the two ---primarily keeping the client's focus on the present, but allowing them to understand the lies that have been spun about their past--- then the client has a clearer understanding of the reality of his or her existence and will better be able to manage the anxiety caused by confronting currently held irrational beliefs.

Both Adler and Ellis approached their treatment methods in high academic fashion. Neither of these methods will facilitate the treatment of a person who has not been educated in a western school system, or a person who did not do well in such a system, or a person who has no use for academia in the first place. They are geared for academics and those who aspire to be academics. This precludes an assumption that the individuals have access to at least middle class incomes and understand the nuances of that social sphere. With the United States poverty level at 15.3 percent, higher than it has ever been and increasing 2.6 percent every five years, this is an assumption that psychologists in the United States cannot afford to make (United States Census Bureau, 2012).

However, when an existential, equal-to-equal philosophy settles between client and therapist, this changes the dynamic entirely. Not only does the academic framework take a back seat to the work it presents, but it relieves the client of any notion that social hierarchy is one of the tools the therapist is using to understand them. A therapist should be able to sit down mano-a-mano with a mechanic or an electrical engineer and they will
both feel un-judged based on their vocations, skill sets, and know how. Existential psychology's philosophical basis provides an avenue where this can happen. If anything, such a situation will provide as much of a challenge for the therapist as it will for the client, and there is no greater continuing

education program than a long-term study of the human condition.

Positive Elements

One of the greatest strengths of this integration is its emphasis on the mind-body connection. Adler's organ inferiority offers a suggestion as to how we can manage physical shortcomings, while the presence of the Umwelt clearly reminds practitioners that not all behavior begins and ends in the mind.

Equally important is this integration's application of history to the present, and its ability to reach to the future. Adlerian interest in historical information not only gives the client a chance to practice rational thought processes – necessary for Ellis's framework to be successful – but it provides the therapist and the client with a more complete picture in the present. Both Adler and the existentialists had an interest in the future, but we can only get there one step at a time, and so Ellis's framework provides that grounding in the present.

Because there is a philosophical acknowledgement of the importance of living at all points in time, this therapeutic model is set up to get the client healthy by taking the time it requires the client to get healthy, no more and no less. There are no time constraints on improvement, but there is a great deal of hope for the future expressed in more than one of these therapy models, and the author believes that this can only help the approach.

Because Adler's therapy model informs REBT and because REBT was designed to interface with cognitive and behavioral therapies when it fell short, this integration should blend well with most therapeutic models. The behavioral elements in Ellis's work allow quick integration with pragmatic models like exposure therapies and interpersonal therapies. Adler's approach ties well with depth therapies such as transactional analysis and brief psychodynamic therapy. Existentialism spreads across the entire approach with a drive for honest existence, no matter how a person gets there. Adler's framework alone provides ample room for maladaptive application. Ellis's framework alone can leave room for fallout if historical issues are not pointedly addressed. Existential psychology provides no framework at all. But when combined, Adler's humanism couples with existentialism's understanding of the human condition and Ellis's pragmatism brings Adler's focus to the present instead of leaving it in the past or flinging it into the future. Conversely, Ellis's pragmatism is tempered by Adler's historical interest and the necessary balance between past, present, and future that is required by existentialism.

Shortcomings

There are unique problems with this form of integrated therapy. First, on its own, it is not a pragmatic method. This would not be an appropriate framework for treating a client suffering from a true psychological emergency – a trauma victim, the survivor of a natural disaster, a floridly expressed schizophrenic, et cetera. Unless the therapist is fully trained in REBT (and that would be the perfect first step toward this integration) or brief psychodynamic therapy, then treating pragmatic issues will present the therapist with some difficulty.

This integration relies heavily on a 'therapist as teacher' framework. Both Ellis and Adler were pointed in this matter; by their standards, it is the therapist's job to steer the client toward reality. Human suggestibility, then, is an issue (Ceci, Bruck, & Loftus, 1998). So is therapeutic misstep (Szentagotai & Kallay, 2006). If the therapist does not adhere to the existential representation of responsibility, where it is clear that the possibility of change rests in the client alone, then there is a greater potential for mistakes –and worse—abuse of power. No amount of training can account for human error, and no amount of accountability can protect a vulnerable client. The existential approach to a therapist's responsibility does not prevent these mistakes, but it does require that a therapist be very mindful of them in a manner that neither Adler nor Ellis overtly advocated.

Conclusion

Because this integration of theories is so versatile, it would be a good framework for any modern-day eclectic therapist. It is respectful of all cultures and blends well with most theistic religious practices and some practices that are not theistic at all. It requires as much awareness from the therapist as it does from the client, and while this may make therapeutic change take a slower route, the result will be a more completely effective philosophy of life when therapy is concluded. In this way, it puts teacher/therapist and client/student on something closer to an even playing field than any other therapy.

Nearly all people have it in their capability to heal, change, and live fully in their respective existences. By presenting therapy in the described manner, clients can be made aware of this fact from the very beginning of treatment. Both Ellis and

Adler put the therapist in a very powerful position, while existentialism places responsibility –and power—solidly with the client. When someone so powerful believes in the client's own strength, whether that strength is initially present or not, the client can be expected to behave as if that strength is as inborn in them as eye and hair color. It's like helping spine trauma victims stand and walk on their own. They might not be able to feel it at first, but the ability is there. It is the therapist's job to help them unlock that ability, and then allow them to create their own balance as they learn to walk back into the world.

References

Batchelder, D. (2006). Recovering a Forgotten Way of Being:

   Church. *Liturgy*, *21*(2), 43-49.

   doi:10.1080/04580630500443621

Bitter, J. B. & Main, F. O. (2011) Adlerian family therapy: An

   introduction. *Journal of Individual Psychology, 67*(3).

Canning, P. (2001). God is Of (Possibility). *Parallax*, *7*(4), 66-88.

   doi:10.1080/13534640110089267

Ceci, S. J., Bruck, M., & Loftus, E. F. (1998). On the ethics of memory

   implantation research. *Applied Cognitive Psychology*, *12*(3),

   230-240.

Daitz, L. (2011). Understanding, Truth or Resolve? *Journal of The*

   Society for Existential Analysis, 22(1), 140-149.

Groth, M. (2010). Cognitive-Behavioural Therapy and Existential

   Analysis. *Existential*

Analysis: Journal Of The Society For Existential Analysis, 21(2), 309-

   319.

Kummerow, J. M. & Maguire, M. J. (2010) Using the myers-briggs

   type indicator frame-work with an adlerian perspective to

increase collaborative problem solving in an organization. *Journal of Individual Psychology, 66*(2).

Matlin, M. (2009). *Cognition.* (7th ed.) Hoboken, NJ. John Wiley & Sons.

Mosak, H. & Fasula, A. (2011) Transference in light of adlerian psychology. *Journal of Individual Psychology, 67*(3).

Mozdzirez, G. J. (2011) Adlerian family therapy: An elusive and controversial challenge. *Journal of Individual Psychology, 63*(3).

Prochaska, J. O. & Norcross, J. C. (2010) *Systems of psychotherapy.* (7th ed.) Belmont,

CA: Brooks/Cole and Cengage.

Rozsnafszky, J. (1974). The impact of Alfred Adler on three 'free-will' therapies of the 1960's. *Journal of Individual Psychology, 30*(1), 65.

Smith, A. (2000). Existential applications to practice: Can existentialism integrate psychotherapy? *Journal of Theoretical and Philosophical Psychology, 20*(1), 80-86. doi: 10.1037/h0091348

Szentagotai, A., & Kállay, É. (2006). The faster you move the longer

    you live – A test of

rational emotive behavior therapy?. Journal Of Cognitive & Behavioral

    Psychotherapies, 6(1), 69-80.

United States Census Bureau. (2012) United states poverty rates

    overview. Retrieved from

    http://www.census.gov/hhes/www/poverty/about/overview/ind

    ex.html

Whitfield, H. J. (2006). Towards case-specific applications of

    mindfulness-based

cognitive-behavioural therapies: A mindfulness-based rational emotive

    behaviour therapy. *Counselling Psychology Quarterly*, *19*(2),

    205-217. doi:10.1080/09515070600919536

Wilberg, P. (2011). From Existential Psychotherapy to Existential

    Medicine. *Existential* Analysis: Journal of the Society for

    Existential Analysis, 22(2), 303-317.

www.ingramcontent.com/pod-product-compliance
Lightning Source LLC
Chambersburg PA
CBHW050520290526
45786CB00007B/2635